THE LONG VIEW

Also By Matthew Kelly

The Dream Manager

Off Balance

Rediscover Catholicism

Why am I Here? (a children's book)

The Four Signs of a Dynamic Catholic

The Seven Levels of Intimacy

Perfectly Yourself

Building Better Families

The Book of Courage

The One Thing

The Rhythm of Life

A Call to Joy

Mustard Seeds

The Shepherd

THE
LONG
VIEW

Some Thoughts About One
of Life's Most Important Lessons

MATTHEW KELLY

Beacon
PUBLISHING

THE LONG VIEW

Printed in the United States of America.[1]

ISBN (Hard Cover): 978-1-937509-74-3

For more information on this title
and other books and CDs available through
the Dynamic Catholic Book Program, please visit:
www.DynamicCatholic.com

The Dynamic Catholic Institute
5081 Olympic Blvd • Erlanger • Kentucky • 41018
Phone: 1-859-980-7900
Email: info@DynamicCatholic.com

*On May 17, 2014, Matthew Kelly
received an honorary doctorate from
Xavier University and was invited
to give the commencement speech.
In the days and weeks that followed,
we received an endless series
of requests for a copy of his remarks
that day. This is his address to the
Class of 2014.*

THE LONG VIEW

This is my advice: Learn to take the long view.

Most people overestimate what they can do in a day, and underestimate what they can do in a month.

We overestimate what we can do in a year, and underestimate what we can accomplish in a decade.

Whatever it is you wish to succeed at in life, personally or professionally, few skills will serve you better than the ability to take the long view.

I say "learn to take the long view" because it is something that has to be learned, for we are constantly surrounded by a short-view mentality in today's culture.

And long view thinking must be practiced constantly, so that it can take root deep in our lives as a well-acquired habit.

For if we wait to reach for it until the day we truly need it, we will find ourselves grasping at air.

What is the long view? It is a
particular brand of wisdom that
takes into account the effects that
something will have not only in the
present but also far into the future.

The Native American people
of the Iroquois have a way of
making decisions that powerfully
demonstrates the long view. When
faced with a decision they ponder
this question: How will this
proposed course of action affect our
people seven generations from today?

It is a beautiful example of taking the long view. One that is in stark contrast to the short-view thinking that our own political leaders seem entrenched in.

When was the last time any of our political leaders considered how their decisions today would affect our people more than one hundred years from now?

And as they are our representatives, we must conclude that they are entrenched in short-view thinking because "we the people" are entrenched in the short-view.

There have certainly been plenty of self-interested politicians in the history of the world – which means that ultimately if enough of the voters demand that our political leaders take the long view, they will adopt it, even if only out of self-interest.

The list of people who have succeeded because they took the long view is long and varied. Henry Ford, Leonardo da Vinci, the Founding Fathers, Alexander the Great, Augustine, Walt Disney, Orville and Wilbur Wright, Albert Einstein, John XXIII, Mozart, Vincent van Gogh, Charles Dickens, Galileo, Socrates, Christopher Columbus, Mother Teresa, Michael Jordan, Winston Churchill, Steve Jobs, Bono, and of course, Ignatius of Loyola and Francis Xavier to name but a few.

Most people are fascinated with the success that taking the long view leads to, but few people adopt it for themselves.

Take as an example the investing philosophy of Warren Buffett.

While I disagree with Mr. Buffett on a great number of things, I cannot dispute his success as an investor. He is arguably the greatest investor of all time and at the core of his success is the long view.

Since 1964, Berkshire Hathaway under the leadership of Buffett has never underperformed the S&P 500 over any five-year interval. If you were given the opportunity to invest ten thousand dollars with Buffett in 1964, and you had the discipline to keep that money invested, by the end of 2012 you would have amassed more than fifty-eight million dollars.

Buffett takes the long view and his success is astonishing. But the average investor owns no shares of Berkshire Hathaway and the average financial professional knows very little about Buffet or his approach, and almost never recommends the stock.

The subject of investing leads us to an immensely practical example of how taking the long view can have an incredible impact on your own life.

You will soon begin your first full-time job. When will you start saving for retirement?

Retirement may seem far off. But taking the long view means taking the far off seriously.

At sixty-five years of age, the average American has a net worth of just $66,740. Sixty-three percent of retired workers in the United States today are dependent on Social Security, friends, relatives, or charity.

If from your twenty-second birthday you save three dollars a day, every day, until your sixty-fifth birthday, you will have saved $47,085. But if you invest those funds at a compounding rate of 9.77%, the historic average market return, at age sixty-five you will have amassed $632,565.

But here's the thing. Most people don't take the long view and most people put off saving for retirement.

Returning to the example, if instead of beginning at twenty-two, you wait just eight years and start saving your three dollars a day from age thirty, leaving everything else in the example the same, at sixty-five you will have less than half as much (or $293,928). Wait until you're forty, keep everything else the same, and you will have a meager $108,625 at sixty-five.

Learn to take the long view, and
learn to take the long view now.

As you make your way through your career the question of compensation will dominate a thousand conversations.

Gather any group of intelligent people together and ask them this question: What determines compensation? What determines how much you get paid?

You will get all the usual answers: education, experience, past performance, networking, market forces, your ability to negotiate, and others. But almost every time this question is discussed one of the largest determinants of compensation is missing from the list.

Your compensation will be
massively impacted by the period
of time you take responsibility
for. Not the period of time you
are given responsibility for, but
the period of time you take
responsibility for.

Consider the compensation
structure at the McDonalds
Corporation.

It is someone's job to get you through the drive-through within three minutes. The period of time that person is responsible for is three minutes. Compensation: minimum wage (or $7.95 an hour in the state of Ohio this morning).

The shift managers are responsible for eight hours. Compensation: roughly twice minimum wage, or $15 an hour.

The store manager is responsible for delivering the monthly results. Compensation: $25 an hour or roughly three times minimum wage.

The franchise owner tends to focus on annual results. Compensation: about $120 an hour, or seventeen times minimum wage, or $250,000 a year.

Then there is the CEO of McDonald's, who's responsible for working out what McDonald's Corporation is doing twenty years from now. Compensation: $25 million last year, or 359 times minimum wage, or $2,853 every hour of every day, even when he is asleep.

Few things will impact your
compensation (and the trajectory of
your career) like the period of time
you spend your energy thinking
about.

Whether it is your job or not, spend fifteen minutes a day thinking about what your organization should be doing ten years from now. And spend fifteen minutes each day thinking about what it is you want to be doing ten years from now.

Develop the habit of thinking far into the future. This is how we learn to take the long view.

The long view has been all around you here at Xavier University. It is one of the reasons this is a place set apart.

In a world where instant gratification isn't fast enough anymore, the need for places dedicated to the long view has never been greater. Xavier is an oasis of the long view.

During your blink-of-an-eye stay here, the campus has been erupting all around you. Every brick in each of these new buildings is a testament to the long view.

The leaders of this community have asked: How can we make the Xavier experience even more powerful for students in the future?

The long view has been all around you here at Xavier because it is at the core of the Jesuit way.

The training of a Jesuit requires more than a decade of study and prayer. This alone is testament that the long view is valued.

Most organizations spend all their energy thinking about today and yesterday, obsessed with solving yesterday's problems and putting out today's fires.

Ignatius began with a long-view vision. He was not interested in short-view thinking. He was committed to building a foundation that would empower great men and women to achieve great things for hundreds of years to come.

More than five hundred years
later, you are the men and women
Ignatius is empowering today to go
out and accomplish great things,
just as he empowered Xavier.

Everything good you have experienced here at Xavier is the fruit of long-view thinking. Just as anything bad you have experienced here is the result of short-view thinking.

But what makes the long-view thinking of Ignatius and Xavier different from the long-view thinking of so many others that the world holds up to be admired? Many men and women throughout history have looked fifty, a hundred, or even a thousand years down the path. But the long-view thinking of Ignatius and Xavier extended into eternity.

If you learn to take the long view, you will find yourself in possession of two of life's most precious commodities: patience and generosity.

Taking the long view teaches us to be patient, and all of life is better for a patient person. Patience will pay immeasurable dividends in your career, marriage, parenting, health and well-being, personal finances, and in your spiritual journey.

Life is relationships. The virtue of patience is the essence of successful relationships. Two patient people will always have a better relationship than two impatient people.

Patience is the fruit of taking the long view. The opposite of being patient is to be frustrated, agitated, intolerant, irritable, restless, and impatient.

Taking the long view also liberates us from selfishness and teaches us to be generous.

Great lives belong to men and women who see life as a generosity contest.

Decide right now, here, today, to live a life of staggering generosity.

Astonish the people who cross your path with your generosity. There is no better way to bring Christianity to life.

Generosity is also the fruit of taking the long view. The opposite of being generous is to be greedy, mean, selfish, stingy, and fearful.

It is patience that allows us to find God in all things, and generosity that sets us free to be men and women for others.

We are all the beneficiaries of Ignatius' bold and staggering generosity here today. We are all the beneficiaries of Xavier's astonishing generosity. How well do you know these men whom you owe so much to as you leave this place today? And what is it that they would want to whisper into your ears this morning? That is the question I pondered in preparing to speak with you.

I have thought long and hard, and I think they would want to pull you close and whisper into your ear: Resist the temptations of short-term gain and instant gratification, and learn to take the long view in all things.

But how do we learn to take the long view? What is required to take the long view? What price does the long view ask us to pay?

Delayed gratification. That's why it's so unpopular. The long view has but one teacher: the intentional postponement of gratification.

So as you begin this next phase of your journey, I ask you: Are you willing to delay gratification?

Nothing will influence your success or failure at anything more than your ability (and willingness) to delay gratification. You simply cannot succeed at anything worthwhile without it.

So, get really good at delaying gratification. Hone this skill. Become a master of this ability and you will become master of yourself.

Have a glass of water when you would rather have a Coke. Force yourself to workout when you would rather not. Wait five minutes before doing something you want to do immediately. Have the fish when you are craving the steak. Take the long way home.

Delayed gratification is the admission price success demands.

The constant denial of self in small things will give you the clarity of heart, mind, and soul to see the present for what it really is and the future for what it still can be.

We read in Proverbs 29:18, "Where there is no vision, the people will perish." People are perishing all around us in society today — perishing in violence, poverty, abuse, selfishness, addiction, loneliness, hopelessness, and exploitation.

Our self-destructive dedication to the short view is impeding our ability to develop a sustainable vision for ourselves, our families, our communities, our nations, and the world.

So, this is my advice: Learn to take the long view.

In a land where there are no
musicians;

in a land where there are no
storytellers, teachers, or poets;

in a land where there are no
men and women of vision and
leadership;

in a land where there are no
legends, saints, or champions;

in a land where there are no
dreamers —

the people of that land will most
certainly perish.

But you and I, we are the music makers;

we are the storytellers, teachers, and poets;

we are the men and women of vision and leadership;

we are the legends, the saints, and the champions;

and we are the dreamers of the dreams.

May God bless you with prayerful spirits, peaceful hearts, and an unwavering commitment to the long view...

and may your lives be filled with love, laughter, and dreams come true.

MATTHEW KELLY has dedicated his life to helping people and organizations become the-best-version-of-themselves! Born in Sydney, Australia, he began speaking and writing in his late teens while he was attending business school. Since that time, four million people have attended his seminars and presentations in more than fifty countries.

Today Kelly is an internationally acclaimed speaker, author, and business consultant. His books have been published in more than twenty-five languages, have appeared on the *New York Times*, *Wall Street Journal*, and *USA Today* bestseller lists, and have sold more than ten million copies.

He is the founder of The Dynamic Catholic Institute, a Cincinnati based non-profit organization whose mission is to re-energize the Catholic Church in America by developing world-class resources that inspire people to rediscover the genius of Catholicism.

Kelly is also a partner at Floyd Consulting, a Chicago based management-consulting firm.

His personal interests include golf, music, literature, spirituality, and spending time with his wife Meggie and their children Walter, Isabel, and Harry.

THE
DYNAMIC CATHOLIC
INSTITUTE

[MISSION]

To re-energize the Catholic Church
in America by developing world-class
resources that inspire people to
rediscover the genius of Catholicism.

[VISION]

To be the innovative leader in the
New Evangelization helping Catholics
and their parishes become
the-best-version-of-themselves.

DynamicCatholic.com
Be Bold. Be Catholic.®

The Dynamic Catholic Institute
5081 Olympic Blvd
Erlanger, KY 41018
Phone: 859-980-7900
info@DynamicCatholic.com